Leave Love, Not Bills
FUNERAL TRUST MADE EASY

By Sara Guida

Copyright © 2025 Sara Guida. All rights reserved.

No part of this publication may be reproduced, distributed, or transmitted in any form or by any means without the prior written permission of the author.

This book is for educational purposes only and does not constitute legal or financial advice. Medicaid and Funeral Trust laws vary from state to state. Readers are encouraged to consult qualified professionals before making financial or legal decisions.

DEDICATION

For every family I've met who wanted to do right by their loved ones but didn't know where to start.

For my children, whom I love dearly. May you always find comfort knowing that your father and I did our best to love and provide for you every single day, even on the hard days.

To my husband, who has stood by my side through thick and thin. Who never tried to change my mind when I took leaps to chase my goals and dreams. I love you deeply.

For my mother, who has always loved me unconditionally and shown me grace without wavering. Her creativity and drive continue to inspire me.

In memory of my father. He was an entrepreneur at heart, driven, courageous, and unafraid to take chances. He taught me that hard work and persistence go hand in hand.

In memory of my grandpa and grandma Smith, who were the most beautiful examples of love and dedication to family. Who showed me unconditional love, resiliency, and kindness.

A NOTE FROM SARA

Planning for death feels heavy.

But what if it could feel like an act of love instead?

Every week, I speak with families who are caught off guard, people who have worked hard all their lives, only to watch their savings disappear on final expenses or long-term care. Many tell me, "I wish we'd known this sooner."

That's why I wrote this book.

You'll learn what a Funeral Trust really is, how it protects your family from last-minute financial stress, and how to set it up the right way. I'll share stories from real people who've used this plan to protect their peace, not just their money.

This isn't about paperwork or policies. It's about peace of mind.

Let's make this simple, human, and doable.

HOW TO USE THIS BOOK

This book is meant to make planning simple, not overwhelming.

You don't have to read it all at once. Use it as a guide you can return to whenever life changes

Start here:

- Read Chapters 1-5 to understand why planning matters and how a Funeral Trust protects both your assets and your family.
- Use Chapter 9's 7-Step Peace of Mind Plan to take action. It guides you through exactly what to do, who to contact, and how to finance your plan.
- Use Chapter 13's Planning Toolkit to organize your documents, store them safely, and share them with those who need to know.

Keep this book in your family records binder or digital vault.

When the time comes, your loved ones will know exactly what to do, and that's the real gift you're giving them.

TERMINOLOGY NOTE

In this guide, the words "Funeral Trust" and "Funeral Expense Trust" are used interchangeably. Both refer to an irrevocable trust that allows you to set aside funds for funeral and burial costs while protecting those assets for Medicaid purposes.

01
PART

Understanding The Why

Before you can plan well, you have to understand why it matters. This section looks at the emotional and financial realities of what happens when families aren't prepared. It's about more than numbers — it's about love, loss, and the peace that comes from knowing your family will be okay when you're gone.

01
CHAPTER

It's Hard to Talk About Dying Until You See Why It Matters.

"Talking about death doesn't bring it closer. Ignoring it doesn't make it go away." - Caitlin Doughty, a well-known mortician, author, and death-positivity advocate (author of "Smoke Gets in Your Eyes" and "From Here to Eternity".

It's Hard to Talk About Dying Until You See Why It Matters.

No one likes to think about dying. Yet one day, each of us will face it. That's a guarantee.

Still, most Americans avoid the topic entirely. According to recent studies, more than half rarely or never think about death. Only about one in five have a written plan.

It's understandable; death feels far away, uncomfortable, or "something for later." But it can arrive suddenly.

And when it does, your family is left to face somewhere between 100 and 200 decisions within the first few days while they're grieving.

Each one feels urgent. Each one comes with emotion and cost.

These are just a few of the decisions that have to be made:

- Where to hold the service
- What kind of casket or urn to choose
- Who will speak or officiate
- What music, readings, or photos to include
- Whether to hold a viewing, visitation, or celebration of life
- How to transport family members and guests
- What flowers, programs, and memorial items to order
- Where to bury or scatter ashes
- How to notify extended family and friends
- How to pay for everything

In the midst of heartbreak, they'll also be asked for payment, as most funeral homes require it up front. Funeral homes often contact families within hours, and they are typically asked to bring specific items to an appointment within the first 24 hours, including a form of payment.

The Hidden Cost of Grief

According to the National Funeral Directors Association, the median cost of a funeral with viewing and burial as of 2023 was $8,300. Add a cemetery plot, headstone, flowers, and travel, and many families pay $10,000–$15,000 or more. When you adjust for inflation and rising costs, a comparable funeral in 2025 could easily cost more.

Life insurance can take weeks to pay out. Most families don't realize that a death certificate is required before the claims process can even begin. Credit cards or loans create new stress. And some families, out of desperation, turn to GoFundMe to cover final expenses.

It's heartbreaking to watch. Families should be grieving, not fundraising.

Why Pre-Planning Matters

Here's the truth:

Every one of us will have a funeral, whether we plan for it or not.

When you plan ahead, you take the weight off your loved ones. You decide your preferences. You set aside funds in advance. You give your family time to mourn instead of scrambling for money.

That's why I believe in the Funeral Trust. It's one of the simplest and most loving tools available, and one of the least discussed.

Let's explore how it works.

CHAPTER

What Is a Funeral Trust?

"A good plan today beats a perfect plan too late."
General George S. Patton

A Funeral Trust (FET) is an irrevocable trust designed for one purpose: to pay your funeral, burial, and all related expenses when the time comes.

Think of it as a dedicated savings plan, protected by law and designed to give your family immediate access to funds when they need them most.

How It Works

You set aside a lump sum typically up to your state's allowable maximum (often $15,000–$17,500, and varies by state). That money funds a single-premium life insurance policy, which is then assigned to the trust.

When you pass away, the insurance company pays the funeral provider directly, typically within 24 to 72 hours once the required documentation is received from the funeral home.

There's no probate, no delays, and no confusion.

Most funeral homes coordinate the paperwork needed for payment, ensuring funds are released quickly and the family can focus on arrangements rather than expenses.

Why It's Better Than a Regular Savings Account Regular savings are considered assets.

A Funeral Trust, however, is protected.

In most states, the funds are:

- ✦ Assets are not counted under Medicaid's spend-down rules
- ✦ Not counted as taxable income
- ✦ Shielded from probate delays or creditors

Your family won't need to pull out a checkbook, call relatives for help, or swipe a credit card. The money is already there, waiting to serve its purpose.

What It Can Cover

The Funeral Trust typically pays for:

- ✦ Funeral home services and professional fees
- ✦ Casket or urn
- ✦ Preparation, cremation, or burial costs
- ✦ Clergy, officiant, or celebrant services
- ✦ Flowers, obituary, and printed materials
- ✦ Transportation and graveside services
- ✦ Celebration of life or memorial gathering expenses

It's flexible enough to honor your wishes without tying you to a specific funeral home.

CHAPTER

Understanding Medicaid and the Spend-Down

"What you don't know about Medicaid can cost you everything you've saved." - anonymous.

Medicaid is a joint federal and state program that helps pay for medical and long-term care for people with limited income and assets.

But here's the catch:

To qualify, you must "spend down" most of your countable assets to $2,000 or less, depending on your state.

That means the savings you worked hard for could disappear quickly, paying for nursing home care, medical bills, or personal expenses.

And how you spend that money matters.

You can't just give it away or hide it. Medicaid reviews your finances for the past five years. This is referred to as the "look-back period." Any unapproved transfers can delay eligibility or result in penalties.

Where the Funeral Trust Fits In

The Funeral Trust is one of the few financial tools recognized by Medicaid as a non-countable asset.

When appropriately structured, the FET allows you to:

- ✦ Protect up to your state's maximum burial amount
- ✦ Qualify for Medicaid more easily.
- ✦ Ensure funeral costs are covered without affecting benefits.

A Real-World Example

Imagine your mom has $52,000 in savings.

Her nursing home care costs $9,000 per month. She'll be broke in six months.

Medicaid won't step in until her assets drop below the state's limit.

By placing $15,000 into a Funeral Trust, she lowers her countable assets and preserves dignity in her final arrangements. Her care is covered, and her family won't be left with unexpected bills. In certain states, it's possible to purchase funeral trusts using a mother's savings for her spouse, her children, and even for a child's spouse though rules vary depending on state law.

That's thoughtful planning, not spending.

04
CHAPTER

Real Families, Real Stories

"Behind every policy and number is a family trying to do the right thing."
-Unknown Author

Case 1: The Son Who Saved His Father's Policy

Mark's father was 84 and living in a care facility. He had an old life insurance policy with a $10,000 face value and $9,800 in cash value, which Medicaid considered an asset.

If he surrendered it, the proceeds would have to be spent down before he could qualify for Medicaid.

Instead, Mark worked with a licensed agent to transfer the policy using a 1035 tax-free exchange into a Funeral Trust, preserving eligibility and ensuring the funds were used for their intended purpose.

The trust turned what could have been a financial problem into a sense of peace of mind.

Case 2: The Mother Who Left a Legacy

Ellen, a widowed mother of seven, entered a nursing home with $141,000 in savings. She wanted to qualify for Medicaid but didn't want to lose everything.

With the help of an advisor, she purchased 14 Funeral Trusts, one for herself, and one for each child and their spouse. This strategy is not available in all states, but in her state, Funeral Trusts can be purchased for spouses, children, and the children of spouses.

She became Medicaid eligible, and when she passed, each family member received a prepaid plan they could use when the time came.

It wasn't just about money. It was a message: I thought ahead because I love you.

Case 3: The Portable Plan

Jack and Linda, both in their early seventies, were planning to retire in Florida. They didn't want to be tied to one funeral home in another state.

They each created a Funeral Trust through a national carrier.

When they moved, nothing changed; their plan was still valid anywhere in the country.

Their family now has clear instructions and immediate funding, no matter where life takes them.

02
PART

Protecting, Planning & Practical Steps

Now that you know why it matters, this section shows you how to make it happen. Here you'll learn exactly how a Funeral Trust works, how to set one up, and how to avoid the most common mistakes families make. It's practical, step-by-step guidance designed to help you take confident action.

05
CHAPTER

Setting Up a Funeral Trust

"Preparation is not morbid. It's merciful." - Unknown Author

Creating a Funeral Trust is simple when you follow the proper steps. Here's precisely how to do it.

Step 1: Secure a Financial Power of Attorney (POA)

Before anything else, ensure a valid financial POA is in place.

This allows a trusted person, usually a spouse, child, or advisor, to make financial decisions on your behalf if you become unable to do so.

Without a POA, your family may face months of court paperwork just to handle your accounts.

> **Quick tip:** Always keep your POA document stored with your trust paperwork and share a copy with your advisor.

Step 2: Work with a Licensed Professional

Funeral Trusts are established through licensed life insurance professionals, financial advisors, or estate planning attorneys who also hold a life insurance license.

Choose someone who:

Understands Medicaid rules.

They should know how spend-downs, exemptions, and look-back periods work in your state. The right advisor will help you avoid costly mistakes and structure the trust correctly so your eligibility isn't delayed or denied.

Works with reputable carriers.

Ensure the company behind your trust is financially stable, has a proven track record of reliability, and specializes in funeral or final expense funding. A trusted carrier ensures your funds are protected and available when your family needs them most.

Can explain everything clearly.

If an advisor can't make the process simple to understand, they probably don't understand it well enough themselves. Choose someone who listens attentively, answers your questions with patience, and makes you feel confident throughout every step of the plan.

Something to watch for: If someone recommends prepaying with a single funeral home, step back and make sure it's genuinely in your best interest. The right plan gives your family freedom and peace of mind, not restrictions.

Step 3: Select the Right Carrier

The trust is funded through a single-premium, guaranteed-issue life policy.

That means:

No medical questions.

There's no health exam, no doctor's visit, and no medical history required. Eligibility is based on age, not health.

Guaranteed acceptance.

Everyone who applies within the eligible age range is accepted. This ensures that even individuals in poor health or in long-term care can still plan ahead.

Available to nearly anyone, ages 0–99.

These policies are designed to help families at every stage of life from parents planning for the future to seniors preparing for a secure retirement.

Because the policy is paid with a single premium, there are no ongoing payments or renewals to worry about. Once the funds are placed, the plan is complete and the trust is active. In some states, policies are also available with flexible payment options over 12, 24, or even 60 months.

When you pass away, the insurance carrier pays the funeral provider directly, usually within 24–48 hours, so your family doesn't have to worry about delays or paperwork.

If you'd like to learn how this type of plan works in your state or explore funding options that fit your situation, contact me. I'll walk you through everything step by step so you can make the best decision for your family.

Step 4: Determine Your Funding Amount

Each state sets its own maximum amount for a Funeral Trust. Many plans allow up to $15,000–$17,500 per person, which varies by state, to be set aside for irrevocable burial funds.

If you're helping someone who is on or near Medicaid eligibility, this number is crucial. It determines how much can be protected from spend-down requirements while still qualifying for care. The right amount ensures their funeral is funded and their savings are preserved.

But even if Medicaid isn't part of your situation, you can still create a plan that fits your personal wishes and budget. Whether that's a modest gathering or a complete celebration of life, you choose what feels right for you and your family.

Think of it as custom peace of mind, a plan that's legally sound, emotionally comforting, and entirely your own.

Step 5: Sign, Assign, and Store Your Documents

Once you complete the policy and assignment forms, you'll receive a Trust Certificate proving that your Funeral Trust is active and funded. This document lists the policy details and the total amount set aside for final expenses.

Keep copies in safe, easy-to-find places:

- One with your advisor or attorney
- One in your family records binder or estate file
- One with your designated Power of Attorney (POA) or trusted family member

And most importantly, tell your family where it is.

A trust can only protect what it's meant to if someone knows it exists. Ensure that your loved ones know who to contact and where to find the necessary paperwork when the time comes.

Consider keeping a small note or card in your wallet or near your essential documents that simply says, "My Funeral Trust is on file. Contact [advisor name or company]." That one detail can save your family hours of searching and ensure everything you planned happens exactly as intended.

Step 6: Review Every Few Years

While a Funeral Trust is irrevocable once it's established, it's still important to review your overall plan if you move to a new state, update your will, or experience significant life changes.

Make sure your advisor or Power of Attorney has up-to-date copies, and confirm that your trust remains aligned with your broader estate and care plans.

PRO TIP: PAIR IT WITH A WILL OR ESTATE PLAN

A Funeral Trust covers funeral costs, but you still need a will or estate plan for everything else. Together, these form a complete protection strategy, one that ensures both your end-of-life wishes and your financial legacy are handled with care.

Your Funeral Trust secures the immediate needs of your service, burial, and final arrangements while a will or estate plan protects everything else: your home, savings, personal belongings, and the people you love.

If you don't yet have a will or estate plan, I strongly encourage you to take that next step. You can visit GetMyWillTrust.com to explore simple, guided planning options that align with your Funeral Trust.

I am not an attorney and do not represent myself as one. My role is to help you understand your options, connect you with trusted resources, and make the planning process easier to begin. You may also contact an estate planning attorney in your state to review your broader legal documents.

The goal is simple: clarity, confidence, and peace of mind for you and relief for your family when they need it most.

CHAPTER

Why Not Just Prepay at a Funeral Home?

"Convenience is great until it locks you in forever." -Unknown Author

Many families are offered prepaid funeral plans directly through a funeral home. They sound appealing: pick your service, pay upfront, and be "done."

But there's a catch. Most prepaid funeral contracts are tied to a single funeral home. That means if you move, change your mind, or the funeral home closes, your family could face major headaches trying to access or transfer those funds.

In some cases, prepaid contracts have limited refund options, hidden fees, or restrictions on how the funds can be used. What once seemed convenient can quickly become confining. That's the danger of confusing convenience with control.

When you prepay a funeral home directly:

+ You're often tied to one location.
+ If you move, your family may not receive full credit elsewhere.
+ If the business closes, changes hands, or mismanages funds, your investment can be at risk.

Real-world cases have shown how prepaid funds were mishandled or lost altogether. Families ended up paying twice or receiving less than promised. (See Endnotes for examples and sources.)

With a Funeral Trust, the funds are portable and flexible. They aren't locked to any funeral home or location. Your family can choose any provider when the time comes. If you relocate or simply change preferences, your trust moves with you—no penalties, no reapplication, no financial surprises.

The goal isn't just to plan. It's to plan wisely.

Real example:

In Missouri, a company named National Prearranged Services (NPS) ran a Ponzi-like prepaid funeral scheme. Many customers paid for plans decades before use, but later discovered the contracts were invalid, mismanaged, or insolvent. https://www.ky3.com/2025/08/05/your-side-investigation-victims-get-checks-prepaid-funeral-scheme

In more recent news, a Connecticut couple prepaid $20,000 for services with a funeral home, only to later learn that funds had vanished. The funeral home operator is now under investigation. https://www.ctinsider.com/journalinquirer/article/pietras-funeral-home-pre-paid-vernon-ct-21062824

In California, state authorities sued funeral homes and master trust operators for misusing millions in "preneed" trust funds, alleging kickbacks, mismanagement, and lack of transparency.

https://oag.ca.gov/news/press-releases/attorney-general-kamala-d-harris-sues-california-funeral-directors-14-million

*This information was accessed 09/2025. Examples are illustrative; laws and outcomes vary by state.

None of this is to say that every funeral home misbehaves. Many are honorable, ethical, and fully operate within guidelines. But when you pay in advance, you're placing trust literally into the hands of a business that may change or fail over time.

That's why a Funeral Trust offers a safer, more flexible path. The funds are held under a controlled structure, your family retains choice, and you avoid the risk of being locked into a single provider or suffering from mismanagement.

The Funeral Trust Difference

When you fund through a life-insurance-backed Funeral Trust, everything changes. You're no longer locked into one location or relying on a single business to "still be there." You're creating flexibility, protection, and peace of mind for your family.

Here's what that looks like in real life:

You choose the provider later.

Your family isn't limited to one funeral home or location. They can select the provider that feels right at the time, whether it's close to home, near a loved one, or in a new state.

Funds are portable nationwide.

Life changes, and so does where we live. If you move, your trust moves with you. The money isn't tied to geography or business ownership. It's available anywhere in the United States.

Insurance company regulations protect money.

The funds are held within a licensed insurance company's trust structure, following strict financial oversight and state regulations. This adds a layer of accountability that most prepaid funeral plans can't match.

Payment is fast and direct.

When the time comes, funds are typically disbursed within 24 to 48 hours and paid directly to the funeral provider. No waiting for a death certificate. No delays from probate. The result?

Why Not Just Prepay at a Funeral Home?

No guessing. No worrying. No dependency on a single business.

Your family will know exactly where the funds are, how to access them, and that every detail you planned has already been taken care of securely, simply, and with dignity.

Prepaid Plan vs. Funeral Trust

Feature	Prepaid Funeral Plan	Funeral Trust
Where funds are held	Held by the funeral home; often tied to one location	Held in a regulated life insurance trust structure
Flexibility	Limited and is often locked to one funeral home	Fully portable – can be used nationwide
Ownership	Controlled by the funeral home or provider	Owned by you; funds designated for your funeral expenses
Protection	May depend on state or business stability	Protected by insurance company regulations and trust law

Feature	Prepaid Funeral Plan	Funeral Trust
Access to funds	May require a claim or transfer process	Paid directly to the funeral provider, usually within 24–48 hours
Risk factors	Subject to business closure, sale, or mismanagement	Secure, portable, and not dependent on any single business
Ideal for	Those who are confident they'll use the same provider long-term	Anyone who values control, protection, and peace of mind

A True Story: The Move That Saved Thousands

Linda prepaid for her funeral in Illinois ten years ago. When she moved to Arizona, she discovered her plan wasn't transferable. The contract was tied to a specific funeral home, and canceling it meant she'd receive only about 60% of her original value back.

If she had used a Funeral Trust, her funds would have remained fully intact and available anywhere in the country because FETs are portable and not tied to any single provider.

Portability equals power. It's the difference between being locked in and staying in control.

Why Some Prepaid Funeral Plans Aren't Transferable

State-specific laws:

Prepaid funeral contracts are governed by state law, and every state regulates preneed (prepaid) funeral funds differently. Some states require that funds be held in a trust account or insurance product, while others allow the funeral home to maintain or manage the funds directly. When a person moves, the new state's rules may not recognize the previous plan's format or guarantees.

Funeral home ownership:

Many prepaid contracts are non-portable because they are tied to a specific funeral home or chain. The funds are often held in trust under that provider's name and can only be redeemed there. If the person moves or the funeral home closes, the only option may be a partial refund, which is often reduced by administrative or cancellation fees (sometimes by 40% or more).

Refund and cancellation clauses:

Most prepaid contracts include a clause stating that if the buyer cancels or relocates, they are entitled to only the cash surrender value, typically 60–80% of the amount paid. This reflects deductions for services, inflation protection, and administrative costs.

No insurance oversight:

Unlike life-insurance-backed Funeral Trusts, prepaid funeral contracts are not always regulated by insurance commissioners. Oversight varies by state, leaving room for inconsistencies and, in rare cases, mismanagement or poor recordkeeping.

Note on Refunds & Protections:

Refund rights and trust protections for prepaid funeral plans vary widely by state. In states like Georgia, preneed sellers are required to deposit full amounts into a trust and honor refunds within three business days (minus minimal fees) if cancellation is requested. https://consumered.georgia.gov/ask-ed/2024-12-04/are-prepaid-funeral-arrangements-refundable *This information was accessed 09/2025. Examples are illustrative; laws and outcomes vary by state.

In other states, only a portion of the funds (sometimes up to 60%) may be required to be placed in a protected account.

Because of this patchwork of laws, it's essential to check your state's statutes or consult a local attorney before signing any prepaid arrangement.

07
CHAPTER

The Numbers That Matter

"Facts bring peace. Guessing brings fear." - Sara Guida

Understanding the numbers behind funeral planning helps you make clear, confident decisions.

Average Funeral Costs 2025 update

(Source: National Funeral Directors Association & U.S. Bureau of Labor Statistics)

Service Type	Median Cost (U.S.)	Notes
Basic service + viewing + burial	$8,300	Doesn't include cemetery or headstone
Cremation with service	$6,280	Excludes urn, niche, or travel
Headstone or marker	$1,500–$3,000	Material and design dependent

Cemetery plot	$2,000–$5,000	Varies by region
Flowers, obituary, transport	$500–$1,200	Often overlooked
Total potential cost	$10,000–$15,000+	Common for full arrangements

Funeral costs continue to rise each year.

According to the National Funeral Directors Association, the median cost of a funeral with viewing and burial increased from $7,181 in 2014 to $8,300 as of 2023. When you include related expenses such as cemetery plots, memorials, flowers, and travel, overall funeral inflation averages between 3% and 4% per year.

Life Insurance Payout Delays

Families often assume life insurance will cover funeral costs, but:

+ Most policies take 14–60 days to pay.

+ First, a death certificate is required. Obtaining a certified copy may take from a few days to several weeks some states report processing times of 12 weeks or more, depending on paperwork, medical review, or local backlog.

+ Once the death certificate is submitted, the claims process begins; however, delays can also occur if the documentation is incomplete or additional review is required.

- Meanwhile, funeral homes typically expect payment up front.

- In some cases, a funeral home may accept a benefit assignment, where the insurer pays them directly; however, this option is not always available and depends on the policy terms and funeral home practices.

That's the gap a Funeral Trust fills.

Medicaid Spend-Down Quick Facts

- Individuals typically must reduce assets to $2,000 or less. This depends on the state in which the individual lives.
- Couples may keep slightly more, depending on the state.
- Gifts or transfers made within the last 5 years can result in penalties.
- Funeral Trusts are generally exempt assets.

Knowing these numbers can prevent thousands in mistakes.

Growth and Value

Most Funeral Trusts grow 0.5%–2.25% per year, not a big profit, but steady. The goal isn't investment growth, it's protection and liquidity.

At a Glance

- Fast payout (24–48 hours)
- Not counted as an asset for Medicaid in most states
- No probate delays
- Simple set up
- State-specific flexibility

Small effort now. Big relief later.

CHAPTER 08

Common Questions Families Ask

"The right answers remove the fear." - Unknown

Below are real questions I hear every week and the simple truths behind them.

Q: Can I set up a Funeral Trust for someone else?

If you have a Power of Attorney, you can establish a Funeral Trust for a loved one.

If you're the policy owner, you can usually set one up for anyone you have a natural insurable interest in, such as a spouse, parent, or child.

Always confirm your state's rules and carrier requirements before funding the trust.

Q: Can I fund it over time?

Most Funeral Trusts are funded with a single premium payment, meaning the plan is paid in full upfront.

However, some carriers allow installment options, typically over 12, 24, or 60 months, depending on availability and state guidelines.

A licensed advisor can review your options and help you choose the best fit for your situation.

Q: What if I move?

No problem. Your Funeral Trust is fully portable across state lines.

You can use any funeral home, anywhere in the United States.

When the time comes, your family simply notifies the provider that payment will be made through the Funeral Trust. The funds are released quickly and directly, no matter where you live.

Q: What happens if I pass away soon after setting it up?

That's a common question, and here's the great news: the full value of your Funeral Trust is available immediately.

There's no waiting period, no penalties, and no delay.

Once the trust is funded and active, your family can access the full amount to cover your funeral expenses whenever they're needed.

Q: Is this taxable?

Benefits used for qualified funeral expenses are generally not taxable. Consult a tax professional for your situation.

When the benefit is used to pay for funeral or burial expenses, it is not taxed to you, your family, or your estate.

The small growth within the trust is also generally tax-free, since it's used for qualified funeral costs.

(Always consult your tax professional for specific situations.)

Q: What if there's money left over after the funeral?

After qualified expenses are paid, any remaining funds go only to the estate of the owner, not to an individual beneficiary.

Families often confuse this with an Estate Planning Trust (EPT), which is separate and allows naming beneficiaries.

EPT assets are generally countable; transfers may be reviewed under the 60-month look-back. After 60 months, prior transfers typically fall outside the review window. To learn more about this option, please see Chapter 11

Q: How fast do funds pay out?

Usually, within 24–48 hours after documentation is submitted to the carrier.

No death certificate delays like traditional life insurance.

Q: Is this legal in every state?

Funeral Trusts are recognized in almost every U.S. state, but the rules and funding limits vary.

Most states allow individuals to set aside $15,000–$17,500 (amounts vary by state) in an irrevocable trust specifically for funeral and burial costs. These funds are considered Medicaid-exempt, meaning they don't count against eligibility for long-term care benefits.

However, a few states handle things differently.

As of this publication, New York and Michigan do not currently approve the use of traditional Funeral Expense Trusts structured through life insurance. These states have their own versions of prepaid or irrevocable burial agreements that must be handled directly with a funeral home or licensed funeral director.

Because every state sets its own rules regarding funding caps and Medicaid recognition, it's important to work with a licensed advisor familiar with your state's regulations. They can confirm the maximum allowable amount and ensure your plan is compliant and protected.

Bottom line: Funeral Trusts are legal and widely accepted nationwide, with only a few exceptions. Always verify your state's current guidelines before funding.

Q: What's the difference between revocable and irrevocable?

A revocable trust can be changed, updated, or canceled at any time by the person who created it. That flexibility can be helpful in some situations, but it also means the assets inside the trust are still considered yours for Medicaid purposes so they're not protected.

An irrevocable trust, on the other hand, cannot be changed once it's established.

The funds are legally removed from your personal assets, which is what allows the plan to qualify for Medicaid exemption.

A Funeral Trust is always irrevocable.

This ensures that the funds are protected, used only for their intended purpose, and not counted toward your Medicaid asset limit.

In short:

- Revocable = flexible but not protected
- Irrevocable = fixed but secure

That's why all properly structured Funeral Trusts are irrevocable by design to guarantee both compliance and peace of mind.

Q: Is this only for seniors?

No. Anyone can set up a Funeral Trust.

While many people use them for senior or Medicaid planning, these trusts can be established at any age, from infants to adults in their nineties.

Parents often create them for adult children, and adult children can establish one for aging parents under a Power of Attorney.

They're also a valuable tool for individuals with special needs, since traditional life insurance or savings could affect eligibility for SSI or Medicaid.

A properly structured irrevocable Funeral Trust allows those funds to be set aside safely without jeopardizing benefits.

In short: Funeral Trusts aren't just for seniors, they're for anyone who wants to plan responsibly and protect loved ones from unnecessary stress.

Q: Can the trust cover cremation?

Absolutely. The trust can fund burial or cremation your choice.

Q: What if I already have a prepaid plan?

That's okay. You can still benefit from a Funeral Trust.

A prepaid plan typically covers the goods and services provided by one funeral home, things like the basic service fee, casket, embalming, or use of facilities. But it often stops there.

A Funeral Trust goes further. It covers everything funeral-related, not just what's offered through one provider. That means:

- Memorial or Celebration of Life events
- Cremation jewelry or keepsakes
- Ash scattering ceremonies or travel expenses
- Family dinners or receptions
- Flowers, programs, and printed materials

In fact, many families use a Funeral Trust to supplement a prepaid plan, especially for the personal touches that make a service meaningful.

If you already have a prepaid plan, your advisor can help you review what's included and determine how a Funeral Trust can fill the gaps. Together, they create a more complete plan that keeps your family fully protected and financially at ease.

In short: The prepaid plan covers the basics.

The Funeral Trust covers everything else the details that make it personal.

Q: Who keeps the paperwork?

You, your Power of Attorney, and a close family member should always have copies of your Funeral Trust paperwork.

You may also choose to share a copy with your advisor or attorney, especially if they assist with your estate or Medicaid planning.

The key is to make sure at least two people know where it's stored and how to access it quickly when needed.

It's also a good idea to include it with your will, trust, or Power of Attorney documents, either in a family records binder, safe deposit box, or digital estate vault.

In short: Keep it safe, keep it shared, and make sure the right people know where it is.

Q: Can I cancel the trust later?

No, because it's irrevocable.

That's what makes it protected under Medicaid rules.

Q: Can Medicaid take this money back?

No. Once funds are in the trust, they're NOT considered assets and used solely for funeral expenses.

Q: Why don't more people know about this?

Because it's not sold by funeral homes or most banks.

It's a niche tool offered by licensed professionals who specialize in long-term care and asset protection.

Q: What's the first step?

Start the conversation.

Talk with your family.

Then reach out to a trusted advisor who can walk you through your options.

03
PART

From Planning to Peace

Planning isn't just about paperwork — it's about leaving love, not bills. This section ties it all together, helping you organize your documents, protect your legacy, and share your plan with the people who matter most. You'll also find guidance for families with special needs, veterans, and professionals who want to help others plan with purpose.

09
CHAPTER

The 7-Step Peace of Mind Plan

"Love is not what you say. It's what you prepare." -Unknown

This is your action plan. Follow these steps and you'll give your family the gift of clarity, not confusion.

1. Confirm or Create Your Financial Power of Attorney (POA)

Without it, no one can legally set up or manage a trust for you once you lose capacity.

A Power of Attorney gives someone you trust the ability to act on your behalf when you can't, ensuring your financial and care decisions stay in the right hands.

If you don't already have one, you can create your Power of Attorney easily and affordably at GetMyWillTrust.com.

It's a simple, guided way to complete the legal forms you need without expensive attorney fees.

Keep a copy with your estate documents and share it with your trusted designee.

This single step can save your family time, stress, and unnecessary expense later.

2. Decide Your Wishes

Burial or cremation? Religious or secular service? Music, flowers, memorial donations?

These are deeply personal choices, and the details matter.

Write them down while you have clarity and control.

Think through:

- Do you want a traditional service, a celebration of life, or something private?

- Are there readings, songs, or people you'd like included?
- Would you prefer flowers or donations to a cause that matters to you?

This isn't morbid, planning it's an act of love. The fewer guesses your family has to make, the more peace they'll have later.

3. Calculate Your Budget

Funeral costs vary widely depending on where you live and what you choose.

Use real numbers to plan wisely.

Start by checking your state's current average cost, usually between $10,000 and $15,000, but in some areas it can exceed $17,000.

Then ask yourself:

- Do I want my trust to cover everything, or just specific items?
- Should I include memorial or travel expenses for family?
- Do I have insurance or savings that might also apply?

Your advisor can help you determine the right amount to fund for your situation.

4. Choose a Licensed Professional

This decision matters. You want someone who knows the rules and respects your goals.

Find a licensed professional experienced in Medicaid planning and Funeral Trusts. Ask them:

- Are you licensed in my state?
- Do you represent multiple carriers or just one?

- Can you clearly explain how Medicaid's spend-down and look-back rules apply?
- How quickly are funds paid out when needed?

If they can't explain it in simple terms, that's a sign to keep looking. You deserve clarity and confidence.

5. Fund the Trust

Most people fund between $10,000 and $15,000.

Your advisor will help assign the single-premium policy to the irrevocable trust.

In some states, monthly payment options are available (12-, 24-, or 60-month plans).

Once it's funded, the trust becomes active ready to do its job when the time comes.

6. Communicate With Family

The best plan in the world is useless if no one knows it exists.

Talk to your loved ones. Tell them:

- That you've set up a Funeral Trust
- Where the documents are stored
- Who to contact when the time comes

You don't have to share every detail, just make sure they know you've prepared. A calm conversation now prevents panic and confusion later.

7. Review and Update

Life changes. So should your plan.

Review your trust every 2–3 years or after major life events like moving, marriage, or loss.

Sall updates keep your plan accurate and your family protected.

Next Step: Organize It All in One Place Once your plan is complete, don't let the details get lost.

Download your Legacy & Final Wishes Planner at LegacyLockPlanner.com to record your wishes, list key contacts, and keep copies of your essential documents together.

It's the perfect companion to your Funeral Expense Trust and will bring your plan full circle.

For detailed guidance on storing, sharing, and securing your documents, see **Chapter 13: Your Planning Toolkit.**

Quick Peace-of-Mind Checklist

Use this checklist to confirm you're fully prepared:

- [ ] I have a valid Power of Attorney (see Step 1)
- [ ] My funeral and memorial preferences are written down.
- [ ] I've confirmed my budget and funding amount.
- [ ] I've chosen a licensed professional I trust.
- [ ] My Funeral Trust is fully funded.
- [ ] My family knows where my documents are.
- [ ] I've reviewed my plan within the last three years.

Remember: Planning ahead doesn't remove emotion; it removes uncertainty.

CHAPTER 10

Final Thoughts: The Last Act of Love

"The best legacy isn't money. It's peace." - Sara Guida

A Funeral Trust isn't about death.

It's about life and the love that keeps protecting even after you're gone.

When you plan ahead, you're not just filling out paperwork. You're lifting a weight your family would otherwise carry in their hardest moment.

You protect your family from unnecessary stress.

You preserve your savings from being spent down.

You leave behind order, not obligation.

This plan becomes more than numbers or forms.

It's your final message to those you love most:

"I cared enough to prepare. You don't have to worry."

Think of it as writing the last love letter your family will ever need to read, written not in words, but in action.

Your Funeral Trust becomes a bridge between your planning and their healing.

Final Thoughts: The Last Act of Love

It gives your family time to remember, to celebrate, and to grieve without financial chaos or confusion.

It's a quiet assurance that your love is still working behind the scenes.

Don't wait for the "right" time.

 here will always be a reason to delay. But the perfect time to create peace is now.

Because the greatest gift you can leave behind isn't wealth it's clarity, care, and calm.

CHAPTER 11

Beyond the Funeral Trust: Understanding Estate Planning Trusts

A Funeral Trust takes care of the immediate and emotional challenge of final expenses. It ensures your funeral, burial, or cremation is paid for quickly, privately, and without burdening your loved ones. But what happens after that?

What if you want to protect your assets for your children, grandchildren, or a favorite charity? That's where an Estate Planning Trust (EPT) comes in.

1. Why This Matters

A Funeral Trust is designed to cover your funeral costs only.

Once the funeral home is paid, any leftover balance does not go to a named beneficiary. It goes back to the estate of the owner, where it becomes part of the probate process. For many families, that's enough. It fulfills a very specific purpose.

But for others, especially those who want to plan beyond the funeral, an Estate Planning Trust adds another layer of peace and purpose.

2. What an Estate Planning Trust Is

An Estate Planning Trust (EPT) is a life-insurance-backed, irrevocable trust designed to:

+ Pass wealth directly to chosen beneficiaries.

- Avoid probate delays and reduce costs.
- Protect the proceeds from creditors.

It's established through a licensed life insurance professional and funded using an existing asset, such as a CD, annuity, or life insurance policy, or through a new single-premium life plan.

This trust type is not immediately Medicaid-exempt, but it gives flexibility for people who aren't seeking Medicaid qualification and still want their legacy protected. The Estate Planning Trust assets are generally countable; transfers may be reviewed under the 60-month look-back. After 60 months, prior transfers typically fall outside the review window.

3. How It Differs from a Funeral Trust

Feature	Funeral Trust (FET)	Estate Planning Trust (EPT)
Purpose	Covers funeral, burial, and final expenses	Distributes assets to beneficiaries, Asset Protection, Tax Preservation, Avoid Probate
Medicaid Treatment	Not considered an asset.	Countable asset (subject to 60-month look-back)

Beneficiaries	Funds go only to the estate	Owner names beneficiaries
Use of Funds	Funeral-related expenses only	First to the Funeral Home, then directly to beneficiaries. The initial claim can be minimal and does not require covering all expenses of the funeral home.
Set up	Simple, single premium, immediate coverage	Simple, single premium, immediate coverage

The two trusts serve different needs but together, they complete the picture.

4. The 60-Month Look-Back Rule

If you're planning for Medicaid eligibility, timing matters.

Most states enforce a 60-month look-back period, meaning Medicaid reviews any asset transfers or new trusts created within the past five years.

If you're setting up an Estate Planning Trust, the funds inside it may delay or impact your Medicaid eligibility until that period passes.

That's why it's essential to understand which trust aligns with your current situation and which may be more suitable later.

5. When to Use Each Trust

- ✦ Use a Funeral Trust if you want to:
- ✦ Protect funds from Medicaid spend-down.
- ✦ Ensure funeral costs are covered immediately.
- ✦ Keep control out of the hands of a single funeral home.

Use an Estate Planning Trust if you want to:

- ✦ Leave a legacy or inheritance for your family.
- ✦ Support a charity or faith-based organization.
- ✦ Avoid probate and control how your assets are passed down.

Many families use both. The Funeral Trust covers end-of-life costs. The Estate Planning Trust continues the story, transferring wealth, values, and peace of mind.

6. How They Work Together

Think of these two trusts as a team:

- ✦ The Funeral Trust protects your family from immediate financial stress.
- ✦ The Estate Planning Trust protects your long-term legacy and allows you to name beneficiaries directly.

Together, they create a plan that covers both today's realities and tomorrow's responsibilities.

7. Where to Get Help

Setting up either trust begins with understanding your goals.

If you're planning for Medicaid or final expense protection, start with a Funeral Trust.

If your goal is to build a lasting legacy and provide gifts or inheritance, an Estate Planning Trust may be the right fit.

You can contact me at FuneralTrustGal.com for more information about how these trusts can work together.

I'm not an attorney and do not represent myself as one. But I can help you understand your options, connect with the right professionals, and take the next step toward peace of mind.

Final Thought

Estate planning isn't just about money. It's about making sure your values, care, and love live on in the way you intended.

With the right plan and the right trust combination, you can leave more than wealth.

CHAPTER 12

Planning for Loved Ones with Special Needs

"Preparation is not about control. It's about care." - Unknown

When you're responsible for a loved one with special needs, you think ahead in ways others may not have to. You plan not just for today but for tomorrow, next year, and long after you're gone.

That's why Funeral Trusts are such a valuable part of special needs planning. They protect both eligibility and dignity.

Why This Matters

Many individuals with disabilities receive benefits such as Supplemental Security Income (SSI) or Medicaid. These programs have strict asset limits, often no more than $2,000 in personal resources.

Even a small inheritance, savings account, or life insurance payout can jeopardize eligibility. The result? Families often spend months trying to fix what could have been prevented with simple pre-planning.

The Safe Way to Plan Ahead

A Funeral Trust is one of the few Medicaid-compliant tools that can be established without incurring a penalty. It allows funds (usually $15,000-$17,500, which vary by state) to be set aside specifically for funeral and burial expenses, and those funds are not counted toward Medicaid or SSI asset limits.

This makes it an ideal solution for:

- Individuals with a Special Needs Trust (SNT) who want to allocate a portion for end-of-life expenses.
- Parents or guardians who want to pre-plan for their child's funeral or future arrangements.
- Guardians, trustees, or fiduciaries who are managing SNT assets and need an approved, safe way to set aside funds.

How It Works

- The trust is funded with a single premium life insurance policy assigned to the irrevocable Funeral Trust.
- The funds are not counted under Medicaid and SSI calculations.
- Upon passing, the money is released directly to the funeral provider, usually within 24–48 hours, ensuring no disruption to benefits or estate distribution.

Case Example: A Legal and Loving Choice

Jessica's parents established a Special Needs Trust for her upon her 18th birthday. It covered her housing, therapies, and care. But they hadn't considered final expenses. Their attorney recommended a Funeral Trust funded through Jessica's SNT. The funds were approved, Medicaid remained intact, and her parents had peace of mind knowing that everything, even the final details, were taken care of.

Unplanned inheritances can also cause issues. Tommy was born with special needs and received Medicaid for his care.

When his uncle passed away, he left Tommy a small inheritance, wanting to help. But that gift unexpectedly jeopardized Tommy's benefits because direct inheritances count as assets.

Working with an advisor, Tommy's parents used part of the funds to create a Funeral Trust. It was approved; Medicaid eligibility stayed intact, and his uncle's gift ultimately brought peace instead of problems. Even good intentions need the right plan.

A Final Act of Love

For families with loved ones who have disabilities, a Funeral Trust is more than financial planning. It's emotional relief. It protects benefits. It preserves independence. And it ensures that no one ever has to worry about how those final costs will be paid. "It's not just smart planning. It's a final act of love and protection."

CHAPTER 13

Your Planning Toolkit

What to Keep, Where to Keep It, and Who to Tell

Keep These Documents Together

Your goal is to make it easy for your loved ones to locate everything they'll need.

Here's what belongs in your planning binder or digital vault:

- Funeral Trust certificate
- Power of Attorney (financial and healthcare)
- Will or estate plan
- Life insurance policies and beneficiary designations
- Funeral or memorial instructions
- Contact list for your advisor, attorney, and funeral provider
- Copies of key identification (driver's license, Social Security card, DD-214 for veterans)

Keep copies of these in two safe locations, such as:

- A fireproof safe at home
- A family records binder
- A secure digital vault

Tip: Make sure at least two trusted people know exactly where to find everything.

Keep It Current

Life changes. Review your documents every few years, or after major life events like:

- Marriage or divorce
- A new home or state move
- Birth of a child or grandchild
- Changes in health or care needs

A quick review ensures that your documents reflect your current wishes and that your loved ones will have the information they need, when they need it most.

Go Digital, Simplify Your Legacy

Paper documents are important, but digital backups make life easier for your family.

That's why I created GetMyWillTrust.com a simple, guided way to set up and store essential legal documents like:

- Wills
- Power of Attorney forms
- Healthcare directives
- Digital estate instructions

You don't need to be an attorney to plan well.

You just need the right tools and someone who cares enough to make it simple.

If you already have your Funeral Trust in place, adding your will and Power of Attorney is the next natural step toward complete peace of mind.

"Planning is an act of love.

Organization is a gift that outlasts you."

Take one small step today, review your documents, share your plan, and secure your legacy.

Simplify Your Legacy

Paper documents are essential, and mapping out the details so your family doesn't have to makes a world of difference to your loved ones.

That's why I created LegacyLockPlanner.com a guided way to record your final wishes, and store everything safely in one place. If you set up your will or trust with me you can upload all these documents into one location using the 15 minute guided set up at GetMyWillTrust.com

Planning well doesn't require an attorney; it just needs someone who cares enough to make it simple.

14
CHAPTER

For Agents and Advisors- Bringing the Funeral Trust to More Families

"The right answers remove the fear."

As an insurance professional, financial advisor, or estate planner, you're in a position to change the conversation.

Too often, clients plan for life but not for death. And yet, this final step is where so many families struggle the most.

Why Agents Should Offer the Funeral Trust

Every client you meet is a potential Funeral Trust opportunity.

Whether they're:

- Helping a parent enter long-term care
- Preparing for retirement
- Managing estate assets
- Working through Medicaid eligibility

A Funeral Trust gives you a simple, compliant, and compassionate solution.

What It Solves for Your Clients

- Immediate access to funds when a loved one passes (no waiting on life insurance claims)

- Medicaid-compliant spend-down option
- Protected, irrevocable funds that can't be misused
- No medical underwriting acceptance from age 0 to 99

It's not about selling another product. It's about solving a problem every family will face.

How to Partner with Me

If you're a licensed insurance professional or an advisor looking to expand your services, I can help you:

- Get appointed with trusted carriers
- Understand state-specific Medicaid rules.
- Integrate Funeral Trusts into your existing client conversations
- Access marketing tools, forms, and training materials
- Learn how to talk about these trusts with confidence and empathy.

"Behind every policy and number is a family trying to do the right thing."

That's the heart of this work. It's not just about money, it's about meaning.

Getting Started

If you're ready to help more families find peace of mind, connect with me directly:

 Sara Guida, Funeral Trust Gal
sara@saraguidaagency.com
FuneralTrustGal.com

You can also learn about my agent training and partnership opportunities through Elder Life Group. Together, we can make responsible planning easier to talk about and accessible to every family.

15
CHAPTER

Veterans and Funeral Trusts

"Service deserves honor. Planning ensures it." — Sara Guida

Veterans give their lives in service to others. It's only right that they receive dignity, respect, and peace of mind in return.

While the U.S. Department of Veterans Affairs (VA) offers several burial benefits, these programs rarely cover the full cost of a funeral or memorial. That's where a Funeral Trust becomes an essential companion to your veteran benefits.

What VA Benefits Cover

The VA provides specific burial benefits for eligible veterans, including:

- A gravesite in a national cemetery
- Opening and closing of the grave
- Perpetual care
- A government-furnished headstone or marker
- A burial flag
- A Presidential Memorial Certificate
- Military funeral honors (if eligible)

These benefits provide tremendous honor and relief for families, but they are limited in scope. They generally do not cover the personal, ceremonial, or family-related costs associated with a full funeral or celebration of life.

What VA Benefits Do Not Cover

Even with VA assistance, the following costs remain the family's responsibility:

- Funeral home professional services and staff fees
- Embalming or cremation
- Transportation of the deceased
- Flowers, obituary, and printed materials
- Memorial service or reception costs
- Family travel or lodging expenses

These expenses can easily add up to thousands of dollars, and most are required to be paid before or during the service.

Where the Funeral Trust Fits In

A Funeral Trust fills the financial gap left by VA coverage.

It ensures that every detail—from transportation to floral arrangements—is funded without burdening your loved ones. The funds are held securely in an irrevocable trust and paid directly to the funeral provider, usually within 24–48 hours of passing.

When structured correctly, a Funeral Trust:

- Works alongside VA burial benefits
- Covers expenses that VA does not pay for
- Is accepted nationwide
- Can protect funds from Medicaid spend-down rules
- Provides immediate access to funds for the family

For Surviving Spouses

Surviving spouses of veterans can also use a Funeral Trust. It allows them to pre-plan their own services while preserving eligibility for Medicaid or other benefits. This ensures that both partners' final arrangements are handled with care, dignity, and financial protection.

In Short

- ✦ VA benefits honor your service.
- ✦ A Funeral Trust honors your family.

Together, they form a complete plan—one that protects your legacy, relieves your family, and ensures your final chapter is handled with the same respect and readiness that defined your life of service.

RESOURCES & TOOLS

Funeral Planning Checklist found on FuneralTrustGal.com

QR Code for quick Access to FuneralTrustGal.com

Document Storage Checklist found on GetMyWillTrust.com

QR Code for quick Access to GetMyWillTrust.com

Set up your Power of Attorney, Will, or Trust by visiting GetMyWillTrust.com

QR Code for quick Access to GetMyWillTrust.com

Get a copy of the End of Life Planner by visiting LegacyLockPlanner.com

QR Code for quick Access to LegacyLockPlanner.com

Conversation Prompts

If starting the conversation feels awkward, try this:

- ✦ "I want to make things easier for you later. Can we talk about my wishes?"
- ✦ "Have you thought about your own plans? I learned something helpful I can share."
- ✦ "Let's spend an hour organizing our family documents together."

Planning is not morbid. It's mercy.

RECOMMENDED NOTES & SOURCES

+ National Funeral Directors Association (NFDA). "2023 General Price List Study." Accessed October 2025.

+ U.S. Department of Veterans Affairs. "Burial and Memorial Benefits." Accessed October 2025.

+ Federal Trade Commission (FTC). "Shopping for Funeral Services." Accessed October 2025.

+ Selected Prepaid Funeral Scandals: NBC News, "Families Left Paying Twice After Prepaid Funeral Funds Mismanaged," 2024. Accessed October 2025.

ABOUT THE AUTHOR

Sara Guida helps families plan ahead for the financial realities of aging, long-term care, and funeral expenses.

As a Funeral Trust Specialist and Founder of the Sara Guida Agency, she works nationwide with clients and professionals to make asset protection simple and compassionate.

Sara believes that knowledge is power and preparation is love.

Connect with her at:

FuneralTrustGal.com

sara@saraguidaagency.com

(402) 769.2485

Follow for educational resources, planning tips, and new tools for families and advisors.

CALL TO ACTION

You've read the guide. Now make your plan.

1. Visit FuneralTrustGal.com for free tools and resources.

2. Download The Funeral Trust Guide directly from my website www.LegacyLockPlanner.com

3. Schedule a 15-minute consultation to get your personalized trust started.

4. Set up your Power of Attorney, Will, or Trust by visiting GetMyWillTrust.com

Don't wait. Protect what matters today.

REQUEST FOR REVIEWS

If this book has helped you or someone you love, please leave a short review on Amazon. Your feedback helps other families find the guidance they need.

www.ingramcontent.com/pod-product-compliance
Lightning Source LLC
Chambersburg PA
CBHW050706160426
43194CB00010B/2025